THE
SPIRITUAL
JOURNAL

Quarterly Devotional System

BY
DR. BILLIE HANKS, JR.
AND BILLY BEACHAM

*"If you are too busy to spend time with God,
you are busier than He intends for you to be."*

Name _____

D1468544

Street Address _____

City _____ ST ___ Zip _____

Phone Number _____

A PERSONAL WORD FROM DR. BILLIE HANKS, JR.

I pray this new *Spiritual Journal* will find a natural and exciting place in your walk with Jesus Christ. My own journals have been constant companions through the years. Many of my fondest memories and deepest insights from the Lord are to be found in their pages. If those insights were ever lost, no amount of money could replace them. Their value is not the kind that money can buy.

When the Lord opens a passage in the Bible to your understanding or teaches you some important lesson through the living of life, you are being entrusted with a pearl of great worth. How should you treat such a pearl? For years, I wasted mine. I forgot the good sermons I heard. I lost the fruit of my quiet times. I left behind the priceless insights gained from my spiritual successes and failures.

One day, God used Matthew 7:6 to convict me! *"Do not give what is holy to dogs, and do not throw your pearls before swine."* He made me see that I was no more mature than the foolish Pharisees, who failed to value that which was holy. Like the dogs and the swine of Jesus' parable, I was wasting and abusing His precious pearls!

Why my life felt empty

God brought me to see why my life felt empty so much of the time. Why should He bless me, when I took His love and fellowship so lightly? Why should I expect Him to teach me? He knew I would only look forward to the next moment of inspiration – never really intending to meditate on my new-found truths or apply them in my daily life.

I began to think I could never break the cycle of spiritual ups and downs. Steady growth seemed impossible! Then slowly but surely things began to change. An older Christian began to disciple me, much as the Apostle Paul helped young Timothy. He showed me the importance of discipline and showed me how to enjoy consistent fellowship with Christ. Life took on a wonderful new dimension!

A "Quiet Time" made the difference

Like so many other Christians, I was delightfully surprised to discover the great difference a daily "quiet time" could make. I learned firsthand what Moses meant in Psalm 90:14, *"O satisfy us in the morning with Thy lovingkindness, that we may sing for joy and be glad all our days."* I experienced His steadfast love in the mornings, and I began to grow.

As time passed, it became natural for me to take notes on my quiet times and the sermons I heard at church. Writing on the back of my bulletin had never been satisfactory, so I began carrying a journal. It grew as I grew, and finally it developed into the *Spiritual Journal* which exists today.

As you begin to use the Quiet Time section, it will also find a special place of importance in your life. When this happens, carefully reserve those special times for fellowship – not work! Your first objective is simply to read your Bible to know God better and experience the joy of His presence.

Be still, as you begin your quiet time. Prepare your heart to listen, and read the Bible expecting a blessing. God will show you more of Himself and His will for your life as He finds that you are teachable. Your Quiet Time section is designed to help you grow in that life-changing process. Maturing in Christ comes as the result of our desire to be consistent. Jesus said, *"If you abide in My Word, then you are truly disciples of Mine."* (John 8:31)

Learning to share

As you enjoy the blessings of Bible reading, prayer, Scripture memory, and note taking, remember to share what you are learning with others. When Jesus called Andrew and Peter, He said, *"Follow Me, and I will make you become fishers of men."* (Mark 1:17) The authenticating mark of true discipleship is the love that causes us to witness. Our commission is to reach out. Jesus said, *"Make disciples of all the nations. . . teaching them to observe all that I commanded you; and lo, I am with you always. . . "* (Matthew 28:19 & 20)

Jesus has not changed! He is still calling men and women to be His committed disciples, not merely His converts. In that awareness, may we take seriously this clear call to be disciplined followers and walk in the joy of His abundant life.

May God bless you and give you real fulfillment as you participate in personal growth and ministry. I pray that this spiritual aid will prove to be a consistent and inspirational part of your Christian life. Let's covenant together to seek to be fully *usable*.

Yours in that expectation,

Billie Hanks, Jr.

"As you therefore have received Christ Jesus the Lord, so walk in Him." (Colossians 2:6)

ABOUT THE AUTHORS

Dr. Billie Hanks, Jr., is president of the International Evangelism Association, Salado, Texas, and has taught and written widely on spiritual growth. The books he has authored and edited include *My Spiritual Notebook, The Christian Discipleship Seminar, Victory Scripture Memory Series, Discipleship, Everyday Evangelism, If You Love Me, A Call to Joy,* and *A Call to Growth.* His books have found popular acceptance with Christian educators, pastors, and lay persons. He also heads The Leadership Training Center for collegiate and seminary men and women, located at West Texas Ranch for Christ near Sweetwater, Texas.

While serving as minister-at-large for the Billy Graham Evangelistic Association in the late 1970s, Dr. Hanks was the featured speaker for area wide pre-crusade conferences on discipleship.

He has traveled in sixty-five countries and participated in congresses on world evangelization in Berlin, Lausanne, Singapore, Minneapolis, and Amsterdam. Teaching from an international perspective, Dr. Hanks is frequently invited to minister on university and seminary campuses.

Billy Beacham is president of Student Discipleship Ministries, Fort Worth, Texas, and serves on several ministry boards including the National Network of Youth Ministries. He ministered ten years with the International Evangelism Association, where he served as vice-president and directed their youth discipleship ministry. Billy is a graduate of Tyler Junior College; University of Texas, Tyler; and Southwestern Baptist Theological Seminary in Fort Worth, TX.

He has authored or co-authored *Back to the Basics, Everyone Everywhere, Growing in Godliness, The True Test, Found Faithful, True Love Waits, Culture in Crisis, My Quiet Time* devotional series, and *The Answer* tract.

Each year over 150,000 high school and college students participate in his discipleship seminars and conferences.

SPIRITUAL JOURNAL

CONTENTS

HOW TO USE THE QUIET TIME SECTION

"Be still, and know that I am God . . ." (Psalm 46:10a, KJV)

1. BEGIN YOUR 15-MINUTE QUIET TIME WITH PRAYER (30 seconds)
   This should be a brief prayer for understanding as you prepare to read God's Word.

2. PAUSE FOR MEDITATION (30 seconds)
   Meditate on the meaning of your memory verse for the week. Repeat it out loud several times, emphasizing the key words which make it meaningful. You may wish to memorize verses from the list found on the back flap of your journal, or find your own verses. (The shaded space at the top of each Quiet Time page is provided for your new memory verse.)

3. READ THE SCRIPTURES (5 minutes)
   You may choose to use the helpful Scripture-reading plan included in your Journal starting on page 88; however, the Quiet Time Section will also work in conjunction with any other plan you select. Regardless of the approach you are led to take, remember that consistency and expectancy are the secrets to spiritual growth in personal devotions.

4. RECORD YOUR SCRIPTURAL INSIGHT, PRAYER, AND PERSONAL APPLICATION (3 minutes)
   Read the Scriptures with personal application in mind. As you look for a Scriptural insight each morning, keep these prayerful attitudes in mind:

   > Lord, help me to . . . (Petition)
   > Lord, You are . . . (Adoration)
   > Lord, thank You for . . . (Thanksgiving)
   > Lord, please forgive me for . . . (Confession)

   (See page 7 for examples.) Seek to make your applications PERSONAL, SPECIFIC, and MEASURABLE. Try to remember a key word or phrase to carry with you throughout the day.

5. SPEND TIME IN PRAYER (2 minutes)
   Start with Adoration, then move to Confession, Thanksgiving, Intercession, and Petition (ACTIP). (Descriptions of these five important aspects of prayer are found on pages 9-13.) Next, pray the prayer that you recorded in your Journal and ask God for strength to carry out the application.

6. REVIEW MEMORY VERSES (4 minutes)
   Review your verses from previous weeks.
   END YOUR QUIET TIME, BUT CONTINUE THE DAY IN PRAYER.

Date: *Jan. 7 - 13*   Memory Verse for the Week: *Psalm 119:11*

"Thy word I have treasured in my heart, that I may not sin against Thee." Psalm 119:11

	Scriptural Insight		Prayer
M O N D A Y	**✱** *1 Peter 1:13* *Don't just slide into the day, meet it aggressively.*	**P**	*Lord, help me to keep my mind centered on You today.*

Application: *I will prepare my mind for Christ-centered thoughts today by meditating on my Quiet Time insight while driving to work rather than listening to the radio.*

T U E S D A Y	**→** *1 Peter 2:13* *I am to be a law abiding citizen, submissive to those in authority.*	**C**	*Lord, please forgive me for consistently breaking the speed limits.*

Application: *Starting today, I will begin driving within the speed limits. Since most of my speeding comes from running late – I will start planning my schedule better.*

W E D N E S D A Y	**m** *1 Peter 3:15* *I need to be ready to witness on any occasion – gently and respectfully.* **✗** *Colossians 4:6*	**P**	*Lord, help me to be disciplined and prepared so I can share the gospel with Sam.*

Application: *This afternoon I will begin committing the Plan of Salvation to memory so I'll be ready when the Lord gives me the opportunity to witness.*

✱	my meditation for today	**A**	Adoration
→	further study needed	**C**	Confession
✗	cross reference	**T**	Thanksgiving
m	verse(s) to memorize	**P**	Petition

SCRIPTURE MEMORY

"Thy word I have treasured in my heart, that I may not sin against Thee."
(Psalm 119:11)

From the earliest days of our faith, long before Bibles could be printed, we were commanded to hide God's Word in our hearts. It was to be the center of our family life and a vital part of every day's experience.

Jesus is our best example for Scripture memory (Matthew 4:1-11). All through His ministry He demonstrated great familiarity with Scripture. He made over 60 specific references to the Old Testament in the four Gospels.

A verse is not truly memorized until you *cannot forget it.* Merely learning a verse is not your spiritual objective – live with the verse until it saturates your mind and affects the way you think and act. Good review is the basis for good meditation, and spiritual meditation produces the kind of thinking that builds a godly life. (Philippians 4:8)

Remember the admonition of Philippians 4:13: *"I can do all things through Him who strengthens me."* This includes hiding God's Word in your heart!

SAMPLE

Date: *Jan. 14 - 20*   Memory Verse for the Week: *2 Corinthians 5:17*
"Therefore if any man is in Christ, he is a new creature; the old things passed away; behold, new things have come." 2 Corinthians 5:17

ADORATION
(Praising God for Who He is)

"I will bless the Lord at all times; His praise shall continually be in my mouth." (Psalm 34:1)

There is no better way to begin a time of prayer than by expressing praise to God! Praise is the most important element of prayer, and it is probably one of the most neglected. In a prayer of adoration, you express your deep feelings toward God in response to His love, wisdom, presence, power, knowledge, grace, holiness, greatness, and His other divine attributes. This kind of prayer will always be an occasion for *joy!*

As you engage in the school of prayer, remember this important lesson: Our adoration must be reserved for God, not for projects, ministries, or works done in His name. When we thank God for what He does, we are gratefully recognizing His answers to our *petitions. Adoration,* on the other hand, focuses on God *Himself* rather than the things He does. As you abide in Him, the desire to praise Him will come naturally.

PRAISING GOD IN ADORATION

The symbol "A" for *adoration* is used in the code provided in the daily Quiet Time prayer section. As you read, you will find many verses which describe God's divine attributes. Make them the subject of your prayer.

	Scriptural Insight	Prayer
S A M P L E	*** 1 Chron. 29:11** In his prayer of adoration, David praised God for His greatness.	**A** Lord, You are the very essence of greatness, power, glory, victory, and majesty. Everything everywhere belongs to You - including me.

Application: I will meditate throughout the day upon who God truly is, and tell Him how proud I am to be His child.

*	my meditation for today	**A**	Adoration
→	further study needed	**C**	Confession
✗	cross reference	**T**	Thanksgiving
m	verse(s) to memorize	**P**	Petition

PETITION
(Praying for Your Personal Needs)

"Until now you have asked for nothing in My name; ask, and you will receive, that your joy may be made full." (John 16:24)

On a day-to-day basis, most of your petitions will deal with small-scale problems, decisions, and opportunities. That is natural, so don't consider your needs beneath God's interest. Remember, Jesus said the Father even knows when a sparrow falls!

Perhaps no verse in the New Testament is as helpful with regard to prayers of petition as John 14:13, in which Jesus said, *"And whatever you ask in My name, that will I do, that the Father may be glorified in the Son."*

In both large and small requests, the question should always be, "Is my prayer the kind that will *glorify* my heavenly Father?"

Pray about everything, and try not to confuse your *needs* with your *wants*. By faith, be prepared to *praise* Him for a "yes" or a "no" when He answers your petition. He knows your need, even before you ask. His promise is wonderfully understandable — *"But seek first His kingdom and His right-eousness; and all these things shall be added to you."* (Matthew 6:33)

BRINGING PETITIONS TO GOD

As you learn to make your requests using the Quiet Time portion of your Journal, indicate your petitions with the symbol "P."

	Scriptural Insight		Prayer
S **A** **M** **P** **L** **E**	→ *Titus 1:7-9 The attributes for spiritual leadership are available to everyone, because they are character qualities that can be developed rather than human talents. This is good news!*	P	*Lord, please help me to have a godly character, so I can be used by You in ministry. Please prepare me for service anyway, anytime, anywhere.*
	Application: *This week I plan to ask Ruth Jones and Frank Spencer what they did to develop the godly character qualities which are so evident in their lives.*		

*	my meditation for today	**A**	Adoration
→	further study needed	**C**	Confession
✘	cross reference	**T**	Thanksgiving
m	verse(s) to memorize	**P**	Petition

CONFESSION
(Agreeing with God about Your Sin)

"If we confess our sins, He is faithful and righteous to forgive us our sins and to cleanse us from all unrighteousness." (1 John 1:9)

Receiving God's gift of forgiveness is part of the miracle that occurs in a person's life when he accepts Christ as Savior. Choosing to accept this gift, made possible through the cross, establishes one's eternal *relationship* with God; however, it is our prayer life and obedience that maintain our *fellowship* with Him on a day-to-day basis.

Jesus said, *"If you love Me, you will keep My commandments."* (John 14:15) When we make self-centered and sinful decisions, our relationship with God remains in effect, but the quality of our *fellowship* is strained. It is *confession* that restores the privilege of that wonderful fellowship.

HOW TO PRACTICE CONFESSION

As you use the daily Quiet Time portion of your Journal, note the single "C" which stands for *confession*. A sincere prayer of confession will normally demand that a practical application be made.

Both sin and righteousness are the result of personal decisions, so *confession* that is based upon *genuine repentance* will be proven by a *change* in your daily life. For this reason, your greatest spiritual victories will normally come as a result of this honest, cleansing kind of prayer.

Your confession and repentance need to be *specific*.

	Scriptural Insight		Prayer
S A M P L E	m *Ephesians 5:15 & 16* *Wise people use their time* *well!*	C	*Lord, please forgive me for* *wasting a lot of time watching* *T.V. lately. These are hours* *I could have spent in Bible* *study, prayer, and service.*
	Application: *I will cut my T.V. viewing back to five hours per week, and spend more quality time with God, my family, and friends.*		
	✱ my meditation for today **➜** further study needed **✗** cross reference **m** verse(s) to memorize		**A** Adoration **C** Confession **T** Thanksgiving **P** Petition

THANKSGIVING
(Expressing Gratitude to God for What He Has Done)

"In everything give thanks; for this is God's will for you in Christ Jesus."
(1 Thessalonians 5:18)

The average Christian probably spends too much time *asking* and too little time *thanking*.

Paul's admonition to *"give thanks in everything"* reflects the maturity of his Christian life. He had been shipwrecked, beaten, hungry, severely criticized, and imprisoned — yet, he could honestly write those words. Why? Because his heart was filled with gratitude! He expressed it like this:

"But whatever things were gain to me, those things I have counted as loss for the sake of Christ. More than that, I count all things to be loss in view of the surpassing value of knowing Christ Jesus my Lord . . ." (Philippians 3:7-8)

Prayer provides the opportunity to express our deepest emotions and feelings to God. How long has it been since your heart was overwhelmed with a sense of gratitude?

OFFERING THANKSGIVING IN PRAYER

As you use the Quiet Time section of your Journal, simply express the natural appreciation in your heart. To indicate your thanksgiving, write "T" in the margin as your code. Begin thanking God for the things in life which you

		Scriptural Insight		Prayer
S	m	*Titus 2:7*	T	*Lord, as I look back over the*
A		*The ministry of example*		*years, I want to thank You*
M		*may be the most important*		*for Sunday School teachers,*
P		*outreach I can have.*		*friends, and family members*
L				*who have been good examples*
E				*for me to follow.*

Application: *I will write a thank-you note to Mrs. Dixon and let her know how much her life has meant to me. I will seek to make my own life a more positive example to others.*

*	my meditation for today	A	Adoration
→	further study needed	C	Confession
✗	cross reference	T	Thanksgiving
m	verse(s) to memorize	P	Petition

INTERCESSION
(Praying for the Needs of Others)

"... far be it from me that I should sin against the Lord by ceasing to pray for you." (1 Samuel 12:23)

When Christ enters our lives, it becomes our spontaneous desire to seek God's blessings for those around us. This is called *intercession*.

It would probably be safe to say that the most consistent intercessory praying which we do focuses on the spiritual needs of relatives, friends, and neighbors. Many of these we intercede for are lost. Others are Christians living beneath the resources and privileges freely available to God's children. In each of these instances, intercessory prayer is a ministry of love.

Through intercession, any Christian can be mightily used of God to affect the cause of evangelism worldwide. Whatever our physical condition, we can all be a part of God's powerful army of prayer. Jesus said to His disciples, *"If you abide in Me, and My words abide in you, ask whatever you wish, and it shall be done for you."* (John 15:7)

INTERCEDING FOR OTHERS

List the names of individuals and ministries that you desire to pray for. When possible, present their needs to God by name. Pray for them exactly as you would want them to pray for you.

The following pages provide space for each day of the week. The example below shows how to use the code at the bottom of the Intercession pages:

		NAME	SPECIFIC REQUEST
S	L	John	Please show him what drinking will do to his life.
A			
M	F	Dad	Give him wisdom in the job decision he is making.
P			
L	C	Mary	Help her as she shares Christ with her grandmother.
E			

F	Family	-	immediate and extended family members
M	Ministries	-	church staff, church services, missionaries, and organizations
C	Close Friends	-	special relationships outside my immediate family
L	Lost Friends	-	those who have not yet come to know Christ as savior
G	Government	-	local, state, and national officials and agencies

INTERCESSION

	NAME	SPECIFIC REQUEST
D A I L Y		
M O N D A Y		

F	Family	-	immediate and extended family members
M	Ministries	-	church staff, church services, missionaries, and organizations
C	Close Friends	-	special relationships outside my immediate family
L	Lost Friends	-	those who have not yet come to know Christ as savior
G	Government	-	local, state, and national officials and agencies

INTERCESSION

NAME	SPECIFIC REQUEST

TUESDAY

WEDNESDAY

F	Family	-	immediate and extended family members
M	Ministries	-	church staff, church services, missionaries, and organizations
C	Close Friends	-	special relationships outside my immediate family
L	Lost Friends	-	those who have not yet come to know Christ as savior
G	Government	-	local, state, and national officials and agencies

INTERCESSION

	NAME	SPECIFIC REQUEST
T H U R S D A Y		
F R I D A Y		

F	Family	-	immediate and extended family members
M	Ministries	-	church staff, church services, missionaries, and organizations
C	Close Friends	-	special relationships outside my immediate family
L	Lost Friends	-	those who have not yet come to know Christ as savior
G	Government	-	local, state, and national officials and agencies

INTERCESSION

NAME	SPECIFIC REQUEST
SATURDAY	
SUNDAY	

QUIET TIME

F	Family	-	immediate and extended family members
M	Ministries	-	church staff, church services, missionaries, and organizations
C	Close Friends	-	special relationships outside my immediate family
L	Lost Friends	-	those who have not yet come to know Christ as savior
G	Government	-	local, state, and national officials and agencies

SPECIAL PRAYER

DATE	PRAYER	DATE ANSWERED

SPECIAL PRAYER

DATE	PRAYER	DATE ANSWERED

QUIET TIME

Date:	Memory Verse for the Week:

	Scriptural Insight	Prayer
M O N D A Y		
	Application:	
T U E S D A Y		
	Application:	
W E D N E S D A Y		
	Application:	

✱	my meditation for today	A	Adoration
→	further study needed	C	Confession
✖	cross reference	T	Thanksgiving
m	verse(s) to memorize	P	Petition

THURSDAY

Application:

FRIDAY

Application:

SATURDAY

Application:

SUNDAY

Application:

Date:	Memory Verse for the Week:

	Scriptural Insight	Prayer
M O N D A Y		
	Application:	
T U E S D A Y		
	Application:	
W E D N E S D A Y		
	Application:	

✱	my meditation for today	A	Adoration
→	further study needed	C	Confession
✖	cross reference	T	Thanksgiving
m	verse(s) to memorize	P	Petition

THURSDAY

Application:

FRIDAY

Application:

SATURDAY

Application:

SUNDAY

Application:

QUIET TIME

Date:	Memory Verse for the Week:

	Scriptural Insight	Prayer

MONDAY

Application:

TUESDAY

Application:

WEDNESDAY

Application:

*	my meditation for today	A	Adoration
→	further study needed	C	Confession
✖	cross reference	T	Thanksgiving
m	verse(s) to memorize	P	Petition

THURSDAY

Application:

FRIDAY

Application:

SATURDAY

Application:

SUNDAY

Application:

Date:	Memory Verse for the Week:

	Scriptural Insight	Prayer
M O N D A Y		
	Application:	
T U E S D A Y		
	Application:	
W E D N E S D A Y		
	Application:	

✱	my meditation for today	A	Adoration
→	further study needed	C	Confession
✖	cross reference	T	Thanksgiving
m	verse(s) to memorize	P	Petition

THURSDAY

Application:

FRIDAY

Application:

SATURDAY

Application:

SUNDAY

Application:

QUIET TIME

Date:	Memory Verse for the Week:

	Scriptural Insight	Prayer
M O N D A Y		
	Application:	
T U E S D A Y		
	Application:	
W E D N E S D A Y		
	Application:	

*	my meditation for today	A	Adoration
→	further study needed	C	Confession
✗	cross reference	T	Thanksgiving
m	verse(s) to memorize	P	Petition

THURSDAY

Application:

FRIDAY

Application:

SATURDAY

Application:

SUNDAY

Application:

Date:	Memory Verse for the Week:

	Scriptural Insight	Prayer
M O N D A Y		
Application:		
T U E S D A Y		
Application:		
W E D N E S D A Y		
Application:		

*	my meditation for today	**A**	**Adoration**
→	further study needed	**C**	**Confession**
✗	cross reference	**T**	**Thanksgiving**
m	verse(s) to memorize	**P**	**Petition**

THURSDAY

Application:

FRIDAY

Application:

SATURDAY

Application:

SUNDAY

Application:

Date:	Memory Verse for the Week:

	Scriptural Insight	Prayer
M O N D A Y		
	Application:	
T U E S D A Y		
	Application:	
W E D N E S D A Y		
	Application:	

✳	my meditation for today	A	Adoration
→	further study needed	C	Confession
✖	cross reference	T	Thanksgiving
m	verse(s) to memorize	P	Petition

THURSDAY

Application:

FRIDAY

Application:

SATURDAY

Application:

SUNDAY

Application:

Date:	Memory Verse for the Week:

	Scriptural Insight	Prayer
M O N D A Y		

Application:

T U E S D A Y		

Application:

W E D N E S D A Y		

Application:

✱	my meditation for today	A	Adoration
➜	further study needed	C	Confession
✖	cross reference	T	Thanksgiving
m	verse(s) to memorize	P	Petition

THURSDAY

Application:

FRIDAY

Application:

SATURDAY

Application:

SUNDAY

Application:

QUIET TIME

Date:	Memory Verse for the Week:

	Scriptural Insight	Prayer
M O N D A Y		
	Application:	
T U E S D A Y		
	Application:	
W E D N E S D A Y		
	Application:	

✱	my meditation for today	**A**	Adoration
➔	further study needed	**C**	Confession
✖	cross reference	**T**	Thanksgiving
m	verse(s) to memorize	**P**	Petition

THURSDAY

Application:

FRIDAY

Application:

SATURDAY

Application:

SUNDAY

Application:

Date:	Memory Verse for the Week:

	Scriptural Insight	Prayer
M O N D A Y		
	Application:	
T U E S D A Y		
	Application:	
W E D N E S D A Y		
	Application:	

✱	my meditation for today	A	Adoration
→	further study needed	C	Confession
✖	cross reference	T	Thanksgiving
m	verse(s) to memorize	P	Petition

THURSDAY

Application:

FRIDAY

Application:

SATURDAY

Application:

SUNDAY

Application:

QUIET TIME

Date:	Memory Verse for the Week:

	Scriptural Insight	Prayer
MONDAY		
Application:		
TUESDAY		
Application:		
WEDNESDAY		
Application:		

*	my meditation for today	A	Adoration
→	further study needed	C	Confession
✖	cross reference	T	Thanksgiving
m	verse(s) to memorize	P	Petition

THURSDAY

Application:

FRIDAY

Application:

SATURDAY

Application:

SUNDAY

Application:

Date:	Memory Verse for the Week:

	Scriptural Insight	Prayer
M O N D A Y		
	Application:	
T U E S D A Y		
	Application:	
W E D N E S D A Y		
	Application:	

✱	my meditation for today	A	Adoration
➜	further study needed	C	Confession
✖	cross reference	T	Thanksgiving
m	verse(s) to memorize	P	Petition

THURSDAY

Application:

FRIDAY

Application:

SATURDAY

Application:

SUNDAY

Application:

QUIET TIME

Date:	Memory Verse for the Week:

	Scriptural Insight	Prayer
MONDAY		
	Application:	
TUESDAY		
	Application:	
WEDNESDAY		
	Application:	

✱	my meditation for today	A	Adoration
→	further study needed	C	Confession
✖	cross reference	T	Thanksgiving
m	verse(s) to memorize	P	Petition

THURSDAY

Application:

FRIDAY

Application:

SATURDAY

Application:

SUNDAY

Application:

NOTE TAKING SECTION

USE YOUR NOTE TAKING SECTION DURING:

Worship Services and Bible Studies

The Journal's approach to note taking is simplified through the use of symbols. When God impresses you with a thought during any part of a sermon, just write it down, code it, and continue note taking. After several weeks, you will become familiar with the symbols. At the end of each message, it will be easy to refer back to the subject areas which have been coded.

Explanation of Symbols:

✱ **Point to Remember:** This could be an outstanding quote, a profound statement, or a new insight from God's Word.

➜ **Further Study Needed:** When you find a passage or thought of particular interest which you would like to study in more detail, code it with an "➜." If the word or passage is unclear, use the same code.

✔ **Illustration:** Summarize good illustrations so you can remember them. You will find that the illustrations God uses to convict or challenge you will often communicate with others as well.

✘ **Cross Reference:** Many times a speaker will refer to related verses in the Bible. In such cases, use an "✘" to code those references. As you become increasingly acquainted with the Scriptures, God will begin bringing references to your mind as you listen to His Word.

○ **Application:** Applying God's Word is the most important principle in living the Christian life. To emphasize areas for application, code your notes with a circle, "○." Notice in the example how the application portions of the notes are circled, as well as coded. You will usually find it necessary to write out specific steps to put your application into immediate practice. Your applications need to be:

> PERSONAL: Select an activity *you* can do!
> SPECIFIC: Be *detailed* and *realistic!*
> MEASURABLE: Give yourself a *time limit!*

"Discipline yourself for the purpose of godliness." (1 Timothy 4:7b)

CODE
* point to remember
✔ illustration
✘ cross reference
→ further study needed
○ personal application

Jan. 16
date

Rev. Jones _1 John 5:11 & 12_
speaker   text

Knowing God
subject/title

☑ Sermon
❑ Sunday School
❑ Bible Study
❑ Book Review
❑ Cassette Tape

"... God has given us eternal life, and this life is in His Son."
- v. 11

* To receive Christ is to begin an eternal relationship with God.

→ "He who has the Son has life. He who does not have the Son of God does not have life." - v. 12.

○ (Lord, I thank You for the eternal life that You have given me.)

* All men are either saved or lost. There is no middle ground!

✔ Salvation resembles marriage. If I ask, "Are you married?" you would not answer, "I hope so," or "Maybe so." Only one of two answers could be correct: "Yes," or "No." The same is true with salvation. Either we have invited Jesus Christ into our hearts as Savior, or we have not.

✘ Jesus said, "I am the way, the truth, and the life. No man comes unto the Father but by Me." (John 14:6) Christ is the only way to heaven!
The message of Christianity is unique. Jesus did not claim to be one prophet among many. He claimed to be God - the only Savior. Because of His death on the cross on our behalf, we can choose to know God as our Father, rather than our judge.

* Every year millions of people die with no knowledge of Jesus Christ.

○ (I need to develop a deeper burden for non-Christians.)

○ (This week I will talk to Mark Green about what it means to be a Christian.)

"... Faith comes from hearing ..."

NOTE TAKING

CODE
* point to remember
✔ illustration
✘ cross reference
→ further study needed
○ personal application

_____ date _____

speaker _____ text

_____ subject/title _____

❏ Sermon
❏ Sunday School
❏ Bible Study
❏ Book Review
❏ Cassette Tape

"... Faith comes from hearing ..."

CODE
* point to remember
✔ illustration
✘ cross reference
→ further study needed
○ personal application

_____ date _____

speaker _____ text

_____ subject/title _____

❑ Sermon
❑ Sunday School
❑ Bible Study
❑ Book Review
❑ Cassette Tape

NOTE TAKING

". . . Faith comes from hearing . . ."

CODE
* point to remember
✔ illustration
✘ cross reference
→ further study needed
○ personal application

date

speaker   text

subject/title

❑ Sermon
❑ Sunday School
❑ Bible Study
❑ Book Review
❑ Cassette Tape

". . . Faith comes from hearing . . ."

CODE
* point to remember
✔ illustration
✘ cross reference
→ further study needed
○ personal application

date

speaker   text

subject/title

❑ Sermon
❑ Sunday School
❑ Bible Study
❑ Book Review
❑ Cassette Tape

NOTE TAKING

". . . Faith comes from hearing . . ."

CODE
* point to remember
✔ illustration
✖ cross reference
➔ further study needed
○ personal application

date

speaker   text

subject/title

❏ Sermon
❏ Sunday School
❏ Bible Study
❏ Book Review
❏ Cassette Tape

". . . Faith comes from hearing . . ."

CODE
* point to remember
✔ illustration
✖ cross reference
→ further study needed
○ personal application

date

speaker   text

subject/title

❏ Sermon
❏ Sunday School
❏ Bible Study
❏ Book Review
❏ Cassette Tape

NOTE TAKING

"... Faith comes from hearing ..."

date

speaker _____ text

subject/title

❑ Sermon
❑ Sunday School
❑ Bible Study
❑ Book Review
❑ Cassette Tape

"... Faith comes from hearing ..."

CODE

* point to remember
✔ illustration
✘ cross reference
→ further study needed
○ personal application

date

speaker _____ text

subject/title

❑ Sermon
❑ Sunday School
❑ Bible Study
❑ Book Review
❑ Cassette Tape

NOTE TAKING

". . . Faith comes from hearing . . ."

CODE
* point to remember
✔ illustration
✘ cross reference
→ further study needed
○ personal application

date

speaker   text

subject/title

❏ Sermon
❏ Sunday School
❏ Bible Study
❏ Book Review
❏ Cassette Tape

". . . Faith comes from hearing . . ."

CODE
* point to remember
✔ illustration
✘ cross reference
→ further study needed
○ personal application

_____ date _____

speaker _____ text

_____ subject/title _____

❏ Sermon
❏ Sunday School
❏ Bible Study
❏ Book Review
❏ Cassette Tape

NOTE TAKING

". . . Faith comes from hearing . . ."

CODE
* point to remember
✔ illustration
✖ cross reference
→ further study needed
○ personal application

_____ date _____

speaker _____ text

_____ subject/title _____

❑ Sermon
❑ Sunday School
❑ Bible Study
❑ Book Review
❑ Cassette Tape

"... Faith comes from hearing ..."

CODE
* point to remember
✔ illustration
✘ cross reference
→ further study needed
○ personal application

date

speaker   text

subject/title

❑ Sermon
❑ Sunday School
❑ Bible Study
❑ Book Review
❑ Cassette Tape

NOTE TAKING

". . . Faith comes from hearing . . ."

CODE
* point to remember
✔ illustration
✘ cross reference
→ further study needed
○ personal application

date

speaker   text

subject/title

❑ Sermon
❑ Sunday School
❑ Bible Study
❑ Book Review
❑ Cassette Tape

". . . Faith comes from hearing . . ."

CODE
* point to remember
✔ illustration
✖ cross reference
➔ further study needed
○ personal application

_____ date _____

speaker _____ text

_____ subject/title _____

❏ Sermon
❏ Sunday School
❏ Bible Study
❏ Book Review
❏ Cassette Tape

NOTE TAKING

"... Faith comes from hearing ..."

- 61 -

CODE
* point to remember
✔ illustration
✖ cross reference
→ further study needed
○ personal application

date

speaker _____ text

subject/title

❏ Sermon
❏ Sunday School
❏ Bible Study
❏ Book Review
❏ Cassette Tape

". . . Faith comes from hearing . . ."

CODE
* point to remember
✔ illustration
✖ cross reference
➜ further study needed
○ personal application

date

speaker   text

subject/title

❑ Sermon
❑ Sunday School
❑ Bible Study
❑ Book Review
❑ Cassette Tape

NOTE TAKING

"... Faith comes from hearing ..."

CODE
* point to remember
✔ illustration
✖ cross reference
→ further study needed
○ personal application

date

speaker   text

subject/title

❑ Sermon
❑ Sunday School
❑ Bible Study
❑ Book Review
❑ Cassette Tape

". . . Faith comes from hearing . . ."

CODE
* point to remember
✔ illustration
✗ cross reference
➜ further study needed
○ personal application

date

speaker   text

subject/title

❑ Sermon
❑ Sunday School
❑ Bible Study
❑ Book Review
❑ Cassette Tape

NOTE TAKING

"... Faith comes from hearing ..."

CODE
* point to remember
✔ illustration
✖ cross reference
→ further study needed
○ personal application

_____ date _____

speaker _____ text

_____ subject/title _____

❑ Sermon
❑ Sunday School
❑ Bible Study
❑ Book Review
❑ Cassette Tape

". . . Faith comes from hearing . . ."

CODE
* point to remember
✔ illustration
✖ cross reference
→ further study needed
○ personal application

_____ date _____

speaker _____ text

_____ subject/title _____

❑ Sermon
❑ Sunday School
❑ Bible Study
❑ Book Review
❑ Cassette Tape

NOTE TAKING

". . . Faith comes from hearing . . ."

date

speaker   text

subject/title

❑ Sermon
❑ Sunday School
❑ Bible Study
❑ Book Review
❑ Cassette Tape

". . . Faith comes from hearing . . ."

CODE
* point to remember
✔ illustration
✘ cross reference
→ further study needed
○ personal application

_____ date _____

speaker _____ text

_____ subject/title _____

❑ Sermon
❑ Sunday School
❑ Bible Study
❑ Book Review
❑ Cassette Tape

NOTE TAKING

". . . Faith comes from hearing . . ."

CODE
* point to remember
✔ illustration
✖ cross reference
→ further study needed
○ personal application

date

speaker   text

subject/title

❑ Sermon
❑ Sunday School
❑ Bible Study
❑ Book Review
❑ Cassette Tape

"... Faith comes from hearing ..."

CODE
* point to remember
✔ illustration
✖ cross reference
→ further study needed
○ personal application

_____ date _____

speaker _____ text

_____ subject/title _____

❑ Sermon
❑ Sunday School
❑ Bible Study
❑ Book Review
❑ Cassette Tape

NOTE TAKING

"... Faith comes from hearing ..."

CODE
* point to remember
✔ illustration
✖ cross reference
→ further study needed
○ personal application

date

speaker _____ text

subject/title

❑ Sermon
❑ Sunday School
❑ Bible Study
❑ Book Review
❑ Cassette Tape

". . . Faith comes from hearing . . ."

CODE
* point to remember
✔ illustration
✘ cross reference
→ further study needed
○ personal application

date _____

speaker _____   text _____

subject/title _____

❑ Sermon
❑ Sunday School
❑ Bible Study
❑ Book Review
❑ Cassette Tape

NOTE TAKING

". . . Faith comes from hearing . . ."

CODE
* point to remember
✔ illustration
✘ cross reference
→ further study needed
○ personal application

date

speaker   text

subject/title

❏ Sermon
❏ Sunday School
❏ Bible Study
❏ Book Review
❏ Cassette Tape

". . . Faith comes from hearing . . ."

CODE
* point to remember
✔ illustration
✖ cross reference
→ further study needed
○ personal application

date _____

speaker _____ text _____

subject/title _____

❑ Sermon
❑ Sunday School
❑ Bible Study
❑ Book Review
❑ Cassette Tape

NOTE TAKING

". . . Faith comes from hearing . . ."

CODE

* point to remember
✔ illustration
✘ cross reference
→ further study needed
○ personal application

date

speaker   text

subject/title

❏ Sermon
❏ Sunday School
❏ Bible Study
❏ Book Review
❏ Cassette Tape

". . . Faith comes from hearing . . ."

CODE
* point to remember
✔ illustration
✖ cross reference
→ further study needed
○ personal application

date

speaker   text

subject/title

❏ Sermon
❏ Sunday School
❏ Bible Study
❏ Book Review
❏ Cassette Tape

NOTE TAKING

". . . Faith comes from hearing . . ."

date

speaker _____ text

subject/title

❑ Sermon
❑ Sunday School
❑ Bible Study
❑ Book Review
❑ Cassette Tape

". . . Faith comes from hearing . . ."

CODE

* point to remember
✔ illustration
✖ cross reference
→ further study needed
○ personal application

date

speaker   text

subject/title

❑ Sermon
❑ Sunday School
❑ Bible Study
❑ Book Review
❑ Cassette Tape

NOTE TAKING

". . . Faith comes from hearing . . ."

CODE
* point to remember
✔ illustration
✘ cross reference
→ further study needed
○ personal application

date

speaker _____ text

subject/title

❑ Sermon
❑ Sunday School
❑ Bible Study
❑ Book Review
❑ Cassette Tape

". . . Faith comes from hearing . . ."

CODE
* point to remember
✔ illustration
✖ cross reference
→ further study needed
○ personal application

date

speaker _____ text

subject/title

❏ Sermon
❏ Sunday School
❏ Bible Study
❏ Book Review
❏ Cassette Tape

NOTE TAKING

". . . Faith comes from hearing . . ."

CODE
* point to remember
✔ illustration
✘ cross reference
→ further study needed
○ personal application

_____ date _____

speaker _____ text

_____ subject/title _____

❏ Sermon
❏ Sunday School
❏ Bible Study
❏ Book Review
❏ Cassette Tape

". . . Faith comes from hearing . . ."

CODE
* point to remember
✔ illustration
✘ cross reference
→ further study needed
○ personal application

date

speaker   text

subject/title

❏ Sermon
❏ Sunday School
❏ Bible Study
❏ Book Review
❏ Cassette Tape

NOTE TAKING

"... Faith comes from hearing ..."

CODE
* point to remember
✔ illustration
✘ cross reference
→ further study needed
○ personal application

date

speaker   text

subject/title

❑ Sermon
❑ Sunday School
❑ Bible Study
❑ Book Review
❑ Cassette Tape

". . . Faith comes from hearing . . ."

CODE
* point to remember
✔ illustration
✘ cross reference
→ further study needed
○ personal application

date

speaker   text

subject/title

❏ Sermon
❏ Sunday School
❏ Bible Study
❏ Book Review
❏ Cassette Tape

NOTE TAKING

". . . Faith comes from hearing . . ."

date

speaker   text

subject/title

❑ Sermon
❑ Sunday School
❑ Bible Study
❑ Book Review
❑ Cassette Tape

". . . Faith comes from hearing . . ."

CODE
* point to remember
✔ illustration
✘ cross reference
→ further study needed
○ personal application

date

speaker   text

subject/title

❑ Sermon
❑ Sunday School
❑ Bible Study
❑ Book Review
❑ Cassette Tape

NOTE TAKING

". . . Faith comes from hearing . . ."

BIBLE READING SCHEDULE

To effectively use the Quiet Time portion of your devotional guide, it is necessary to have a plan for consistent daily Bible reading. Plan to read at a pace that is comfortable for you. Strive for understanding and not just quantity.

Start by reading Matthew 1:1-17 during your first daily quiet time. Continue reading successive passages each morning and check the ☑ box for that day. You may wish to break these reading segments into smaller portions by stopping at each new Scripture insight which you find. May you continue to grow spiritually as you let God mold your character through His Word!

Matthew	Matthew (cont.)	Matthew (cont.)	Matthew (cont.)
❑ 1:1-17	❑ 8:23-27	❑ 16:13-20	❑ 25:1-13
❑ 1:18-25	❑ 8:28-34	❑ 16:21-28	❑ 25:14-30
❑ 2:1-12	❑ 9:1-8	❑ 17:1-13	❑ 25:31-46
❑ 2:13-18	❑ 9:9-13	❑ 17:14-23	❑ 26:1-13
❑ 2:19-23	❑ 9:14-17	❑ 17:24-27	❑ 26:14-30
❑ 3:1-12	❑ 9:18-26	❑ 18:1-9	❑ 26:31-35
❑ 3:13-17	❑ 9:27-34	❑ 18:10-14	❑ 26:36-46
❑ 4:1-11	❑ 9:35-38	❑ 18:15-20	❑ 26:47-56
❑ 4:12-17	❑ 10:1-16	❑ 18:21-35	❑ 26:57-68
❑ 4:18-22	❑ 10:17-31	❑ 19:1-12	❑ 26:69-75
❑ 4:23-25	❑ 10:32-42	❑ 19:13-15	❑ 27:1-10
❑ 5:1-12	❑ 11:1-19	❑ 19:16-30	❑ 27:11-26
❑ 5:13-16	❑ 11:20-24	❑ 20:1-16	❑ 27:27-44
❑ 5:17-20	❑ 11:25-30	❑ 20:17-19	❑ 27:45-56
❑ 5:21-26	❑ 12:1-14	❑ 20:20-28	❑ 27:57-66
❑ 5:27-30	❑ 12:15-21	❑ 20:29-34	❑ 28:1-15
❑ 5:31-32	❑ 12:22-37	❑ 21:1-11	❑ 28:16-20
❑ 5:33-37	❑ 12:38-45	❑ 21:12-17	
❑ 5:38-42	❑ 12:46-50	❑ 21:18-22	**Mark**
❑ 5:43-48	❑ 13:1-23	❑ 21:23-27	❑ 1:1-12
❑ 6:1-4	❑ 13:24-30	❑ 21:28-32	❑ 1:13-20
❑ 6:5-15	❑ 13-31-35	❑ 21:33-46	❑ 1:21-28
❑ 6:16-18	❑ 13:36-43	❑ 22:1-14	❑ 1:29-34
❑ 6:19-24	❑ 13:44-46	❑ 22:15-22	❑ 1:35-39
❑ 6:25-34	❑ 13:47-52	❑ 22:23-33	❑ 1:40-45
❑ 7:1-6	❑ 13:53-58	❑ 22:34-40	❑ 2:1-12
❑ 7:7-12	❑ 14:1-12	❑ 22:41-46	❑ 2:13-17
❑ 7:13-14	❑ 14:13-21	❑ 23:1-7	❑ 2:18-22
❑ 7:15-23	❑ 14:22-36	❑ 23:8-12	❑ 2:23-28
❑ 7:24-29	❑ 15:1-20	❑ 23:13-36	❑ 3:1-6
❑ 8:1-4	❑ 15:21-28	❑ 23:37-39	❑ 3:7-12
❑ 8:5-13	❑ 15:29-39	❑ 24:1-14	❑ 3:13-30
❑ 8:14-17	❑ 16:1-4	❑ 24:15-35	❑ 3:31-35
❑ 8:18-22	❑ 16:5-12	❑ 24:36-51	❑ 4:1-20

Mark (cont.)

- ❏ 4:21-25
- ❏ 4:26-29
- ❏ 4:30-34
- ❏ 4:35-41
- ❏ 5:1-20
- ❏ 5:21-43
- ❏ 6:1-6
- ❏ 6:7-13
- ❏ 6:14-29
- ❏ 6:30-44
- ❏ 6:45-56
- ❏ 7:1-23
- ❏ 7:24-30
- ❏ 7:31-37
- ❏ 8:1-13
- ❏ 8:14-21
- ❏ 8:22-26
- ❏ 8:27-30
- ❏ 8:31-38
- ❏ 9:1-13
- ❏ 9:14-32
- ❏ 9:33-37
- ❏ 9:38-50
- ❏ 10:1-12
- ❏ 10:13-16
- ❏ 10:17-31
- ❏ 10:32-45
- ❏ 10:46-52
- ❏ 11:1-11
- ❏ 11:12-19
- ❏ 11:20-26
- ❏ 11:27-33
- ❏ 12:1-12
- ❏ 12:13-17
- ❏ 12:18-27
- ❏ 12:28-34
- ❏ 12:35-40
- ❏ 12:41-44
- ❏ 13:1-13
- ❏ 13:14-31
- ❏ 13:32-37
- ❏ 14:1-11
- ❏ 14:12-26
- ❏ 14:27-31
- ❏ 14:32-42
- ❏ 14:43-52
- ❏ 14:53-65
- ❏ 14:66-72

Mark (cont.)

- ❏ 15:1-15
- ❏ 15:16-20
- ❏ 15:21-32
- ❏ 15:33-41
- ❏ 15:42-47
- ❏ 16:1-8
- ❏ 16:9-20

Luke

- ❏ 1:1-25
- ❏ 1:26-38
- ❏ 1:39-45
- ❏ 1:46-56
- ❏ 1:57-66
- ❏ 1:67-80
- ❏ 2:1-20
- ❏ 2:21-40
- ❏ 2:41-52
- ❏ 3:1-20
- ❏ 3:21-38
- ❏ 4:1-13
- ❏ 4:14-30
- ❏ 4:31-37
- ❏ 4:38-44
- ❏ 5:1-11
- ❏ 5:12-16
- ❏ 5:17-26
- ❏ 5:27-32
- ❏ 5:33-39
- ❏ 6:1-11
- ❏ 6:12-16
- ❏ 6:17-26
- ❏ 6:27-36
- ❏ 6:37-42
- ❏ 6:43-45
- ❏ 6:46-49
- ❏ 7:1-10
- ❏ 7:11-17
- ❏ 7:18-23
- ❏ 7:24-35
- ❏ 7:36-50
- ❏ 8:1-15
- ❏ 8:16-18
- ❏ 8:19-21
- ❏ 8:22-25
- ❏ 8:26-39
- ❏ 8:40-56
- ❏ 9:1-9

Luke (cont.)

- ❏ 9:10-17
- ❏ 9:18-27
- ❏ 9:28-36
- ❏ 9:37-45
- ❏ 9:46-50
- ❏ 9:51-56
- ❏ 9:57-62
- ❏ 10:1-24
- ❏ 10:25-37
- ❏ 10:38-42
- ❏ 11:1-13
- ❏ 11:14-28
- ❏ 11:29-32
- ❏ 11:33-36
- ❏ 11:37-54
- ❏ 12:1-12
- ❏ 12:13-21
- ❏ 12:22-34
- ❏ 12:35-48
- ❏ 12:49-59
- ❏ 13:1-9
- ❏ 13:10-17
- ❏ 13:18-21
- ❏ 13:22-30
- ❏ 13:31-35
- ❏ 14:1-14
- ❏ 14:15-24
- ❏ 14:25-35
- ❏ 15:1-7
- ❏ 15:8-10
- ❏ 15:11-32
- ❏ 16:1-18
- ❏ 16:19-31
- ❏ 17:1-10
- ❏ 17:11-19
- ❏ 17:20-37
- ❏ 18:1-8
- ❏ 18:9-14
- ❏ 18:15-17
- ❏ 18:18-30
- ❏ 18:31-43
- ❏ 19:1-10
- ❏ 19:11-27
- ❏ 19:28-44
- ❏ 19:45-48
- ❏ 20:1-19
- ❏ 20:20-26
- ❏ 20:27-40

Luke (cont.)

- ❏ 20:41-47
- ❏ 21:1-4
- ❏ 21:5-38
- ❏ 22:1-13
- ❏ 22:14-38
- ❏ 22:39-46
- ❏ 22:47-53
- ❏ 22:54-62
- ❏ 22:63-71
- ❏ 23:1-25
- ❏ 23:26-43
- ❏ 23:44-56
- ❏ 24:1-12
- ❏ 24:13-35
- ❏ 24:36-53

John

- ❏ 1:1-18
- ❏ 1:19-28
- ❏ 1:29-34
- ❏ 1:35-42
- ❏ 1:43-51
- ❏ 2:1-11
- ❏ 2:12-25
- ❏ 3:1-21
- ❏ 3:22-36
- ❏ 4:1-26
- ❏ 4:27-38
- ❏ 4:39-42
- ❏ 4:43-54
- ❏ 5:1-15
- ❏ 5:16-30
- ❏ 5:31-47
- ❏ 6:1-15
- ❏ 6:16-24
- ❏ 6:25-59
- ❏ 6:60-71
- ❏ 7:1-13
- ❏ 7:14-24
- ❏ 7:25-44
- ❏ 7:45-52
- ❏ 8:1-11
- ❏ 8:12-30
- ❏ 8:31-41
- ❏ 8:42-59
- ❏ 9:1-12
- ❏ 9:13-34
- ❏ 9:35-41

ADDITIONAL AIDS

Galatians (cont.)
- ❏ 3:15-29
- ❏ 4:1-7
- ❏ 4:8-20
- ❏ 4:21-31
- ❏ 5:1-15
- ❏ 5:16-26
- ❏ 6:1-10
- ❏ 6:11-18

Ephesians
- ❏ 1:1-14
- ❏ 1:15-23
- ❏ 2:1-10
- ❏ 2:11-22
- ❏ 3:1-13
- ❏ 3:14-21
- ❏ 4:1-16
- ❏ 4:17-32
- ❏ 5:1-21
- ❏ 5:22-33
- ❏ 6:1-9
- ❏ 6:10-24

Philipians
- ❏ 1:1-11
- ❏ 1:12-30
- ❏ 2:1-18
- ❏ 2:19-30
- ❏ 3:1-11
- ❏ 3:12-21
- ❏ 4:1-9
- ❏ 4:10-23

Colossians
- ❏ 1:1-14
- ❏ 1:15-23
- ❏ 1:24-29
- ❏ 2:1-12
- ❏ 2:13-23
- ❏ 3:1-17

Colossians (cont.)
- ❏ 3:18-25
- ❏ 4:1-6
- ❏ 4:7-18

1 Thessalonians
- ❏ 1:1-10
- ❏ 2:1-12
- ❏ 2:13-20
- ❏ 3:1-13
- ❏ 4:1-12
- ❏ 4:13-18
- ❏ 5:1-11
- ❏ 5:12-28

2 Thessalonians
- ❏ 1:1-12
- ❏ 2:1-12
- ❏ 2:13-17
- ❏ 3:1-15
- ❏ 3:16-18

1 Timothy
- ❏ 1:1-11
- ❏ 1:12-20
- ❏ 2:1-15
- ❏ 3:1-16
- ❏ 4:1-16
- ❏ 5:1-10
- ❏ 5:11-25
- ❏ 6:1-10
- ❏ 6:11-21

2 Timothy
- ❏ 1:1-18
- ❏ 2:1-13
- ❏ 2:14-26
- ❏ 3:1-9
- ❏ 3:10-17
- ❏ 4:1-8
- ❏ 4:9-22

Titus
- ❏ 1:1-16
- ❏ 2:1-15
- ❏ 3:1-15

Philemon
- ❏ 1:1-25

Hebrews
- ❏ 1:1-14
- ❏ 2:1-4
- ❏ 2:5-18
- ❏ 3:1-6
- ❏ 3:7-19
- ❏ 4:1-13
- ❏ 4:14-16
- ❏ 5:1-10
- ❏ 5:11-14
- ❏ 6:1-12
- ❏ 6:13-20
- ❏ 7:1-10
- ❏ 7:11-28
- ❏ 8:1-13
- ❏ 9:1-10
- ❏ 9:11-28
- ❏ 10:1-18
- ❏ 10:19-39
- ❏ 11:1-40
- ❏ 12:1-13
- ❏ 12:14-29
- ❏ 13:1-25

James
- ❏ 1:1-18
- ❏ 1:19-27
- ❏ 2:1-13
- ❏ 2:14-26
- ❏ 3:1-12
- ❏ 3:13-18
- ❏ 4:1-12
- ❏ 4:13-17

James (cont.)
- ❏ 5:1-12
- ❏ 5:13-20

1 Peter
- ❏ 1:1-12
- ❏ 1:13-25
- ❏ 2:1-12
- ❏ 2:13-25
- ❏ 3:1-7
- ❏ 3:8-22
- ❏ 4:1-11
- ❏ 4:12-19
- ❏ 5:1-14

2 Peter
- ❏ 1:1-11
- ❏ 1:12-21
- ❏ 2:1-12
- ❏ 2:13-22
- ❏ 3:1-18

1 John
- ❏ 1:1-10
- ❏ 2:1-14
- ❏ 2:15-29
- ❏ 3:1-10
- ❏ 3:11-24
- ❏ 4:1-6
- ❏ 4:7-21
- ❏ 5:1-12
- ❏ 5:13-21

2 John
- ❏ 1:1-13

3 John
- ❏ 1:1-14

Jude
- ❏ 1:1-16
- ❏ 1:17-25

After you have completed these New Testament Quiet Time reading segments, you can enjoy reading one chapter per morning from Proverbs and Psalms. Next, start with Genesis and read one chapter per day as you move through the Old Testament. Finally, plan to read Revelation which is the last book of the Bible.

CODE		WITNESSING
P	Personal Testimony	**OPPORTUNITIES**
BI	Bridge Illustration	
EB	Evangelistic Booklet	*"For I am not ashamed of the gospel, for it is*
ET	Evangelistic Tape	*the power of God for salvation to everyone*
B	Bible Given Away	*who believes."* (Romans 1:16)

Date	Code	Description	Code

NEXT ACT ON MY PART

FOLLOW-UP MINISTRY

letter	l
phone call	p
personal visit	v
other	o

"Sharing from the spiritual overflow"

PERSONAL MINISTRY ACTIVITIES
FOR THE MONTH OF _____

SUNDAY	MONDAY	TUESDAY	WEDNESDAY	THURSDAY	FRIDAY	SATURDAY

ADDITIONAL AIDS

PERSONAL MINISTRY ACTIVITIES
FOR THE MONTH OF _____

	SUNDAY	MONDAY	TUESDAY	WEDNESDAY	THURSDAY	FRIDAY	SATURDAY

PERSONAL MINISTRY ACTIVITIES
FOR THE MONTH OF _____

SUNDAY	MONDAY	TUESDAY	WEDNESDAY	THURSDAY	FRIDAY	SATURDAY

ADDITIONAL AIDS

PERSONAL MINISTRY ACTIVITIES
FOR THE MONTH OF _____

SATURDAY	FRIDAY	THURSDAY	WEDNESDAY	TUESDAY	MONDAY	SUNDAY